The Illustrated Laws of
SOCCER

By George Fischer
Illustrated by Patrick T. McRae

Ideals Children's Books • Nashville, Tennessee
an imprint of Hambleton-Hill Publishing, Inc.

Published by Ideals Children's Books
An imprint of Hambleton-Hill Publishing, Inc.
Nashville, Tennessee 37218

Printed and bound in Mexico

Library of Congress Cataloging-in-Publication Data
Fischer, George, 1952–
    The illustrated laws of soccer / by George Fischer ; illustrated by Patrick T.
McRae.
      p.   cm.
    ISBN 1-57102-020-9
    1. Soccer—Rules—Juvenile literature. [1. Soccer—Rules.] I. McRae,
Patrick, ill. II. Title.
GV943.4.F655   1994
796.334'02'022—dc20   94-1910
                                    CIP
                                    AC

Reviewed and endorsed by the United States Soccer Federation.

Table of Contents

Note to Parents:

This book was designed to communicate the basic laws of soccer and to stimulate expanded discussion of the game.

To standardize soccer rules and promote international play, an organization called FIFA (Fédération Internationale de Football Association) was formed. Its headquarters are in Zurich, Switzerland. Most youth soccer teams play under rules that are based on the Laws of the Game as defined by FIFA, but that are modified in order to promote greater participation by young players.

These pages present the FIFA Laws of the Game in simplified form so that they can be easily understood by young soccer players. Information was selected on the basis of what would be of most interest to young players and parents and most suitable for discussion. Modifications of the laws for youth games are indicated.

This book offers an excellent way to capture and hold the interest of young soccer players, to inform them of important points of the game, and to facilitate discussion of the game by players and their parents.

The Game of Soccer

The game of soccer is the most popular sport in the world. It had its beginnings long ago, before the time of recorded history. It is thought that the game developed in England and then spread throughout the world. It is the national sport of many countries, including most European and Latin-American nations.

The game was originally called "football" because players move a ball down a playing field with their feet. In England and many other nations, the game is still called football, or "association football." In some countries such as the United States and Canada, the game is called "soccer," which comes from the abbreviation for "association."

During a soccer game, a team of players tries to kick or strike a ball into the other team's goal. This team must also try to keep the other team from kicking or striking a ball into its own goal. One thing that makes the game interesting is that no player, except the goalkeeper, is allowed to touch the ball with his or her hands. Players must move the ball either by kicking it with their feet or by striking it with their heads or bodies. The team that makes the most goals wins the game.

The most important prize in soccer is the World Cup. This is a tournament which is held every four years and in which many countries enter a national team. The tournament is played using the "Laws of the Game."

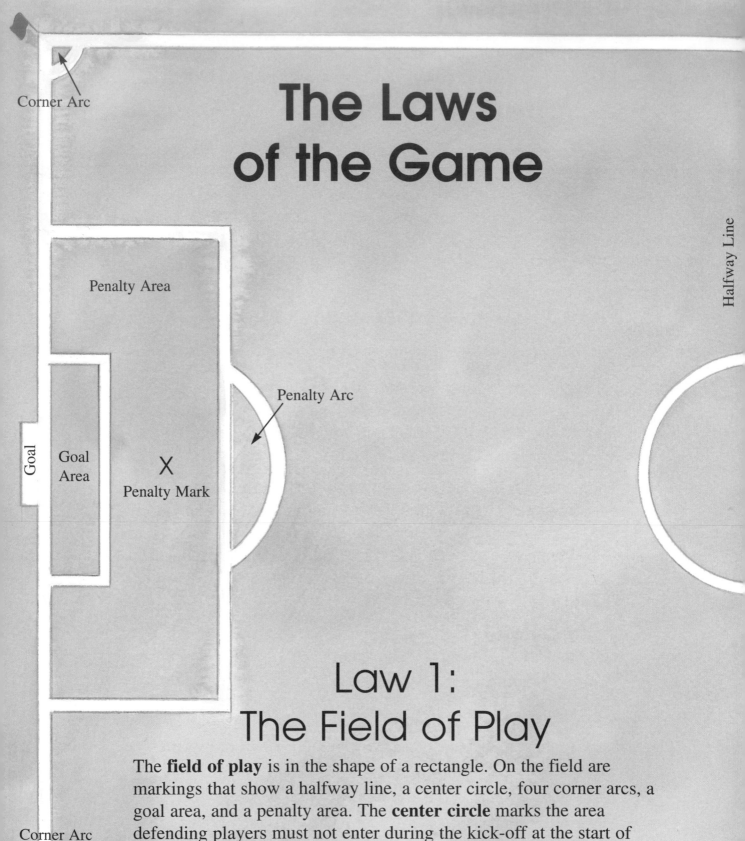

Corner Arc

Penalty Area

Halfway Line

Penalty Arc

Goal

Goal
Area

X
Penalty Mark

Corner Arc

The Laws
of the Game

Law 1:
The Field of Play

The **field of play** is in the shape of a rectangle. On the field are markings that show a halfway line, a center circle, four corner arcs, a goal area, and a penalty area. The **center circle** marks the area defending players must not enter during the kick-off at the start of the game. A player awarded a corner-kick (see Law 17) makes the

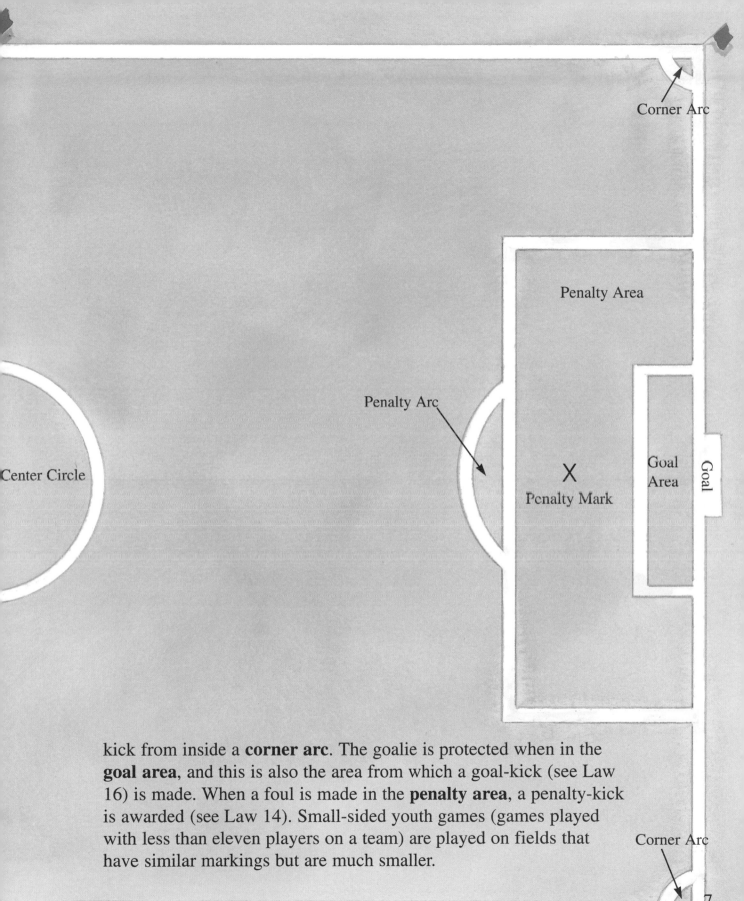

Corner Arc

Penalty Area

Penalty Arc

Center Circle

X
Penalty Mark

Goal
Area

Goal

Corner Arc

kick from inside a **corner arc**. The goalie is protected when in the **goal area**, and this is also the area from which a goal-kick (see Law 16) is made. When a foul is made in the **penalty area**, a penalty-kick is awarded (see Law 14). Small-sided youth games (games played with less than eleven players on a team) are played on fields that have similar markings but are much smaller.

Law 2: The Ball

The official ball is 27 to 28 inches in **circumference** (the distance around the outside of the ball) and weighs 14 to 16 ounces. This is a Size 5 ball. Younger players should play with a smaller ball, one that is Size 4 or Size 3.

Law 3: Number of Players

The maximum number of players a team may have on the field at any one time is eleven. One of these players must be the goalkeeper. Some youth soccer teams play with smaller numbers of players. These are called small-sided games. Games may be played with seven players (called seven-sided) or four players (called four-sided) on a team.

BILLY G.   FORWARD

RYAN M.   FORWARD

MIKE G.   FORWARD

MARIA R.   MIDFIELDER

JIMMY L.   MIDFIELDER

ALEXA M.   MIDFIELDER

EMILY M.   DEFENDER

TONY T.   DEFENDER

ZACH L.   DEFENDER

AJ   SWEEPER

MIGUEL A.   GOALIE

Law 4: Players' Equipment

A player's equipment includes a jersey, shorts, socks, shinguards, and shoes. The goalkeeper must wear colors that are different from the colors of the other players and the referee.

Law 5: Referee

The referee enforces the laws of the game. The referee's decisions are final.

Referee

Linesman

Law 6: Linesmen

Linesmen help the referee. They tell the referee when the ball is out of play (out-of-bounds), which team should put the ball back into play, and when a player substitution is needed. They also help the referee to identify fouls and misconduct. The referee may overrule the linesmen.

Linesman

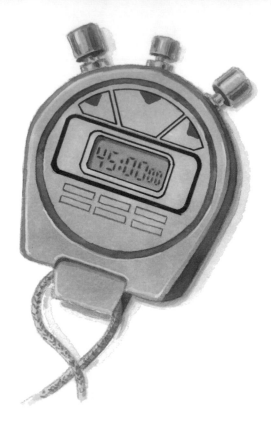

Law 7: Duration of Game

The official game of soccer is played in halves. Each is forty-five minutes long and there are five minutes between halves. Many youth games are played with shortened halves. For example, a four-sided youth game may be played in four twelve-minute quarters with a five-minute halftime break and two-minute breaks between quarters.

Law 8: The Start of Play

All players must start on their own half of the field. Defending players must be at least ten yards from the ball. (Some rules for youth soccer teams allow defending players to be eight yards from the ball, or six yards for even younger players.) The ball must be kicked forward from the center of the field. The ball is said to be **in play** after it has traveled the distance of its own circumference.

Law 9: Ball In and Out of Play

The ball is in play until it has gone completely out-of-bounds, unless the game is stopped by the referee for another reason.

Ball in bounds

Ball out-of-bounds

Law 10: Method of Scoring

The entire ball must cross the goal line into the goal in order to score.

The team that scores the most goals is the winner.

A game may end in a tie.

Goal Line

This player is off-side

Law 11: Off-Side

A player is in an **off-side** position if the player is closer than the ball is to the opponent's goal line—unless

- the player is on his or her own side of the field

   OR

- two opponents are as near to the goal line as the player is.

This is considered a foul only when the player in this position is a part of the play, then the referee will call a penalty.

A player will not be called off-side when he or she receives the ball directly from a throw-in, a corner-kick, or a goal-kick.

The off-side rule should not be enforced in small-sided youth games.

Law 12: Fouls and Misconduct

If a player commits one of the following nine fouls, the other team is given a **direct free-kick** (see Law 13):

1. Kicking an opponent.
2. Tripping.
3. Jumping at an opponent.
4. Charging in a dangerous way.
5. Charging from behind, unless the opponent is obstructing (see below).
6. Striking or spitting at an opponent.
7. Holding an opponent.
8. Pushing.
9. Handling the ball (except for the goalkeeper when in his or her own penalty area).

If a player commits one of the following five fouls, the other team is given an **indirect free-kick** (see Law 13):

1. Playing in a way the referee considers dangerous.
2. Charging, even if fairly, when the players involved are not trying to play the ball.
3. When not playing the ball, intentionally running between an opponent and the ball (called **obstructing**).
4. Charging the goalkeeper, except when the goalkeeper is holding the ball, is obstructing, or is outside his or her own penalty area.
5. When playing as the goalkeeper within his or her penalty area, playing in a way that holds up the game and wastes time, or taking more than four steps while holding the ball.

Law 13: Free-kicks

Direct free-kick: This kick may be made and a goal scored without the ball first touching another player.

Indirect free-kick: The goal may not be scored unless the ball touches another player after the kick is made.

Law 14: Penalty-kick

A **penalty-kick** is awarded when a defending player commits a "direct free-kick" foul (see Law 12) within his or her own penalty area. This means the ball is put back into play by the attacking team with a kick made from the defender's penalty mark, with only the goalie defending the goal.

Penalty Mark

Law 15: Throw-in

When the ball goes out of play over a sideline, the ball is put back in play with a **throw-in**. The thrower must keep both feet on the ground, use both hands, and throw the ball from a position behind the head.

Law 16: Goal-kick

When the attacking team plays the ball out-of-bounds over the goal line, the defending team puts the ball back in play with a **goal-kick** made from inside the goal area. The ball may not be played again until it has passed outside the penalty area.

Law 17: Corner-kick

When the ball is played out-of-bounds over the goal line by the defending team, the ball is put back into play by the attacking team with a **corner-kick** made from inside a corner arc.

21

The Players

Forward

Defender

Forward

Midfielder

Defender

Defender

Midfielder

Goalkeeper

Defender

Forward

Midfielder

Soccer is very much a team sport. In soccer, when your team has the ball, everyone on your team is an offensive player. When the other team has the ball, everyone on your team is a defensive player.

Soccer players on an eleven-sided team may start a game in positions such as those shown in the illustration. Once the game begins, the positions should change as the players move about the field.

Players on youth teams should be encouraged to play a variety of positions in order to gain valuable experience. A player may be called a forward, a midfielder, a defender, or a goalie. On the next few pages are descriptions of the skills that are desirable for each of these positions. It's important to remember that any player may take the ball to the goal, and every player should defend his or her own goal.

23

The Forward

A **forward,** or **striker,** is a primary goal scorer. A forward should be quick, have good ball control skills, and should be able to kick the ball accurately.

The Midfielder

A **midfielder** must have strong endurance to go after free balls, to support offensive runs, and to drop back quickly to defend when the other team gains the ball.

The Defender

A **defender** must slow down the opponent's attack and use his or her body position to force the play away from the goal. This player must have good timing in order to separate the ball from the attacker without fouling. Although this player is called a defender, he or she also needs good passing and dribbling skills for times when it is necessary to attack.

The Goalkeeper

The **goalkeeper,** or the **goalie,** is the only player on the team who can use his or her hands to play the ball. It is good for this player to be quick, agile, and aggressive in order to get to the ball.

Referee Signals

Arm Straight up in the Air

This is the signal that an **indirect free-kick** is being awarded.

Arm Held out Straight

This is the signal that a **direct free-kick** is being awarded.

Linesman Signals

Flag Signal

This signals that the ball is **out-of-bounds.**

Flag in Circular Motion

This signals that a **foul** has been made.

Sportsmanship in the Game of Soccer

While winning is an important part of competition, it is even more important to think about fair play and fun while developing the basic skills and knowledge of the game.

The *players* are expected to follow the Laws of the Game, to pay attention to the referee's warnings, and to show respect to all others, on and off the field, including members of the opposing team. This kind of behavior is known as good sportsmanship.

The *coach* is responsible for the behavior of the players, the assistant coaches, the players' parents, and for his or her own behavior. The coach sets the standards of sportsmanship for the team by his or her own actions, by how the players are coached, and by explaining to the parents what is expected of them.

The *spectators,* who are parents for the most part, should remember that they are there to enthusiastically support the players. They are not there to coach the players or to criticize the players or the officials. Their most valuable contribution is to help make the soccer game a fun-filled experience for all.

The *referee* will penalize players for unsportsmanlike conduct, dangerous play, continued breaking of the laws, or showing opposition to an official's call. The referee may stop the game to warn a coach about his or her conduct or to ask the coach to restrain the parent group. The referee may ask a person who is displaying poor sportsmanship to leave the field.

To emphasize the positive aspects of sportsmanship, many youth soccer tournaments give a special award to the team whose players, coaches, and parents best exhibit good sportsmanship throughout the tournament.

Summary of the Laws of Soccer

Law 1: The Field of Play
The field of play is in the shape of a rectangle. Markings show a halfway line, a center circle, four corner arcs, a goal area, and a penalty area.

Law 2: The Ball
The official ball is 27 to 28 inches in circumference. A youth team may play with a smaller ball.

Law 3: Number of Players
A team has no more than eleven players on the field, one being the goalkeeper. Youth teams often play with fewer players.

Law 4: Players' Equipment
The goalkeeper must wear colors that are different from those of the other players.

Law 5: Referee
The referee enforces the laws of the game. The referee's decisions are final.

Law 6: Linesmen
Linesmen help the referee make decisions.

Law 7: Duration of Game
The official game of soccer is played in two halves, each forty-five minutes long. Youth games may be played in quarters or with shortened halves.

Law 8: The Start of Play
All players must start on their own half of the field. Defending players must be at least ten yards from the ball. The ball must be kicked forward from the center of the field. The ball is said to be "in play" after it has traveled the distance of its own circumference.

Law 9: Ball In and Out of Play
The ball is in play until it has gone completely out-of-bounds, unless the game is stopped by the referee for another reason.

Law 10: Method of Scoring
The entire ball must cross the goal line into the goal in order to score. A game may end in a tie.

Law 11: Off-Side
A player is in an off-side position if the player is closer than the ball is to the opponent's goal line—unless the player is on his or her own side of the field or two opponents are as close to the goal line as the player is. Some youth leagues do not enforce the off-side law.

Law 12: Fouls and Misconduct
Kicking, pushing, tripping, and holding players is not allowed. No player may play the ball with the hands, except for the goalkeeper. If a foul is committed, the other team is given a free-kick.

Law 13: Free-kicks
Direct free-kick: This kick may be made and a goal scored without the ball first touching another player.
Indirect free-kick: The goal may not be scored unless the ball touches another player after the kick is made.

Law 14: Penalty-kick
A penalty-kick is awarded if a foul is committed by a defending player in his or her own penalty area.

Law 15: Throw-in
When the ball goes out of play over a sideline, the ball is put back in play with a throw-in. The thrower must keep both feet on the ground, use both hands, and throw the ball from a position behind the head.

Law 16: Goal-kick
When the attacking team plays the ball out-of-bounds over the goal line, the defending team puts the ball back in play with a goal-kick.

Law 17: Corner-kick
When the ball is played out-of-bounds over the goal line by the defending team, the ball is put back into play by the attacking team with a corner-kick.

Vocabulary of the Game

center circle: a circle with a 10-yard radius marked around the center mark on the halfway-line; defending players must stand outside this circle at kick-off

charge: to run directly to a ball in an attempt to win it, or gain possession of it, from an opponent

dribbling: moving the ball down the playing field with the feet

free ball: a ball when it is not under the control of or in the possession of a player

hand ball: a foul in which a player purposefully touches the ball with his or her hands or arms

"playing" the ball: moving the ball by striking it with the player's head, body, or feet

marking: guarding a member of the opposing team

obstructing: when not playing the ball, to intentionally run between an opponent and the ball

save: to prevent the ball from going into the goal

small-sided game: a youth game in which teams play with fewer than eleven players on a side (four- or seven-sided teams are common)

tackle: to use the feet or shoulder to take the ball away from a member of the opposing team

trap: to use the feet, thighs, or chest to get control of the ball

volley: a kick made to the ball while it is in mid-air